P9-DHJ-083
God's
PROMISES
to a Woman's Heart
25 DAILY DEVOTIONS
Jane L. Fryar

The mission of CTA is
to glorify God by providing purposeful products
that lift up and encourage the body of Christ—
because we love him!

www.CTAinc.com

God's Promises to a Woman's Heart

by Jane L. Fryar

1625 Larkin Williams Rd., Fenton, MO 63026

PRINTED IN THAILAND

All Your Needs

Have you ever gotten news too good to be true?

This week you will read promises sent directly from God's heart to your heart. They are very good. Best of all, they are completely true.

Rest in them!

Day 1
No Half-Measures!

My God will meet all your needs according to his glorious riches in Christ Jesus.
Philippians 4:19

You know what half-measures are. You come home from work hungry and tired. You rummage around in the refrigerator but find only the light bulb. Sighing, you stir up a bowl of oatmeal.

If you're tired enough and if you can sprinkle some brown sugar on top, the oatmeal may meet your need for sustenance. But it's a half-measure, at best. How much more satisfying a hearty bowl of soup, some fruit, and two slices of homemade bread with raspberry jelly would be!

We rely on half-measures when time or money or both make us reluctant to go all out. We also rely on half-measures when we're reluctant to commit ourselves—from the heart. Halfhearted commitment leads to half-measures. Can failure follow far behind?

With that in mind, reread the verse from Philippians quoted above. Not one hint of half-measures here! Paul, inspired by the Holy Spirit, makes a wonderful promise. It comes from God's heart to our ears. And it brings peace. We need not fear. All of our needs will be met—and not stingily, but "according to God's glorious riches"!

So how rich is God? He built the universe! All the diamonds in all the mines on earth and in every distant galaxy belong to him! All the gold. All the silver. All the real estate in every star system. All the knowledge. All the wisdom.

But that's not the end. The riches we've been promised are "in Christ Jesus." God is not rich just in material things. First and most important, he's rich in love—in love for you and me! He showed it by sending Jesus to die for us and rise again. If he gave his Son into death, will he withhold any other good thing from us? Certainly not!

This book includes readings based on 25 all-inclusive promises from God himself. None describes half-measures. Nor does our Savior-God make any of them halfheartedly. He's fully committed to you—in Christ Jesus.

Lord, I sometimes take half-measures in my walk with you. But you never befriend me halfheartedly. Teach me to trust all you've promised in Christ Jesus . . .

I will bless her with abundant provisions; her poor will I satisfy with food.
Psalm 132:15

Are you easy to satisfy? hard to please?

If your dog sits, shakes hands, and rolls over, are you content? Or would you prefer that he speak Japanese and prepare Belgian waffles for breakfast at least one day a week?

If your landlord cleans the carpets once every two years and sends you a Christmas card, are you tickled pink? Or do you expect a new oven when the handle wiggles loose?

Those are, of course, ridiculous examples of what it might take to create satisfaction. No landlord would go to those lengths. And not even earth's smartest canine could!

Now that you're thinking about satisfaction, though, reread Psalm 132:15 (above). The Lord addresses these promises to his people, the Church. And what promises they are! He will grant abundant provision. He will satisfy the poor with food.

Many Scriptures promise that God will provide the food, clothing, and shelter his people need. These verses, though, promise something else. The context makes it clear that

Psalm 132:15 refers to spiritual needs. The words of the psalm echo those of our Lord Jesus in Matthew 5:3–6.

Blessed are the poor in spirit,
for theirs is the kingdom of heaven. . . .
Blessed are those who hunger and thirst for
righteousness, for they will be filled.

We are "poor in spirit" when we recognize our deep poverty before God, when we realize the debt we have incurred by our sins. The hymn writer put it this way: "Nothing in my hands I bring, simply to thy cross I cling." Our guilt before God is very bad news, but God's promise of "abundant provision" brings hope!

We "hunger and thirst for righteousness"—a righteousness we can't buy, earn, or prepare. And in our Savior, those yearnings are satisfied. Because of all that Jesus did for us, we can look forward to heaven's eternal banquet hall. And right now here on earth, our Lord's provision comforts and sustains us. It's an all-inclusive, awesome promise!

Lord Jesus, my need is deeper than I can know. But your gracious provision for me in the cross goes far beyond my need. Satisfy my . . .

I will refresh the weary and satisfy the faint.
Jeremiah 31:25

By some estimates, seven of every ten doctor visits are fatigue-related. That's a lot of weariness! Sometimes fatigue is a symptom of disease. But fatigue has other sources, too. Long-term stress. Grief. Ongoing frustration. Clinical depression. The list of causes goes on and on.

Always, though, fear and worry make weariness worse. Anyone who has lain awake at night stewing about an aging parent, a straying spouse, or a child with autism knows how quickly fear and worry can dig a pit—and how deep and dark that pit can be.

Into our darkness the Lord shouts his promise to refresh us. Far more helpful than a splash of cold water on tired eyes, far more effective than two pots of stiff coffee, God's promise touches our hearts, planting seeds of hope. "I will refresh the weary," he says.

A tall lemonade on a hot day. That first dive into the pool after the cover comes off in spring. A care package from home during finals week at college. These things refresh us.

How much more refreshing, though, to see a friendly face, to hear a loved one's voice, to receive a hug from someone who cares deeply about us. The presence of those we love during life's lonely, troubled times—now that's refreshing!

And how much more so when the one who comes to refresh our souls is the Savior, who loved us to death—his own death on the cross!

At times we find ourselves as innocent bystanders in the troubles that engulf us. At other times, we have caused the train wreck of our circumstances. (Or, at least, contributed to it.) But always, Jesus comes to forgive and heal, to refresh and satisfy our hearts with his love for us. In the light of his promise, worries melt and fears shrink.

Are you "fainting" today from weariness? Are you struggling with an unresolved illness? Are you carrying a burden of guilt or fear or worry? Whatever the cause of your fatigue, pause and invite your Savior to refresh your soul.

Lord, you refresh me by your presence and in your promises. Teach me to rely more and more on you, especially . . .

Day 4
First Things First

Seek first his kingdom and his righteousness, and all these things will be given to you as well.
Matthew 6:33

Imagine you've moved into a new house or apartment. What would you unpack first? Probably not the Christmas tree ornaments or the shoe polish or the bridesmaid's dress you wore in your sister's wedding a decade ago.

In Matthew 6:31–33, Jesus urges us toward a first-things-first lifestyle. Then he identifies our "first things" for us: "Seek first [God's] kingdom and his righteousness," our Lord says.

What would it mean to seek God's kingdom first? We see the answer—in perfection—as we reflect on the life of our Lord Jesus: loving God by loving people.

This was no syrupy, soap-opera love. This love went way beyond expectations to care for those in need. This love told the truth, never mind the consequences. This love refused to be manipulated. This love took our Lord into uncomfortable situations, and it created unlikely relationships.

What's more, Jesus' love was by no means cheap. In the end, he paid the ultimate price, an unimaginable price. Jesus' love—his love for you and me—cost him his life!

Our Savior died for those times we focus on ourselves rather than on him. He died because we choose to chase after second and third and fourth things. He died for our cowardice in "being nice" when real love would "be honest." He died for the times we've done what was convenient rather than what was best for the other person.

And now, Jesus calls us, his forgiven daughters, into his own first-things-first lifestyle. We may feel timid about stepping out into that kind of risky, self-giving love. But we can do it, knowing we will never walk alone. He walks right beside us, filling us with peace and leading the way.

We can lay aside our worries about every detail, right down to what we'll eat or drink or wear. He promises, "All these things will be given to you as well" (Matthew 6:33). It's an all-inclusive promise by our ever-loving Lord!

Dear Jesus, you love me, and you'll never stop loving me. It's amazing! Be my first thing and my only thing as you teach me to love others . . .

He will deliver the needy who cry out, the afflicted who have no one to help.
Psalm 72:12

I have a coupon in my wallet. It entitles me to a free latte at my favorite coffee shop. I've had the coupon for a month, and I visit the shop at least twice a week. But I keep forgetting to use the coupon.

This past week, as I've reflected on the promises of God, I've thought a lot about my unredeemed coupon and about our Lord's promises. How often we fail to cash in on the plain promises of Scripture—even when we're desperate for help. Why is that?

Perhaps we see our Savior as a kind of divine insurance agent. We'll call on him for life's major crises, but we have decided not to "bother him" with the little details of daily living. If so, our relationship with him suffers.

Or perhaps we like to project an image of ourselves as "superwoman" at work, in our family and circle of friends, and even at church. Maybe that cloak has become so familiar, we wear it even into our heavenly Father's presence when we pray. If so, our relationship with him suffers.

On the other hand, perhaps the promises of Scripture seem just too good to be true. Maybe we've heard "experts" explain them all away, stealing our confidence in some intellectual sleight of hand. If so, our relationship with our Lord suffers.

Why would God make such extravagant, all-encompassing promises if he didn't intend to keep them? And why would we try to hide our vulnerabilities or explain away the wonder of his power active in love on our behalf?

Perhaps the most common reason for our prayerlessness is simply that we forget. Jesus' promises—promises greater than any others—simply fall off the radar of our busy lives. This, too, gets in the way of the dynamic, growing relationship our Savior wants to have with us.

Awareness is the first step in overcoming roadblocks to both prayer and unshakable confidence in the promises of God. You've just taken that step. So now, ask already!

Lord, your promises are rich and wonderful! Forgive my faithlessness and fearfulness. Listen now as I cry out. You're my only help . . .

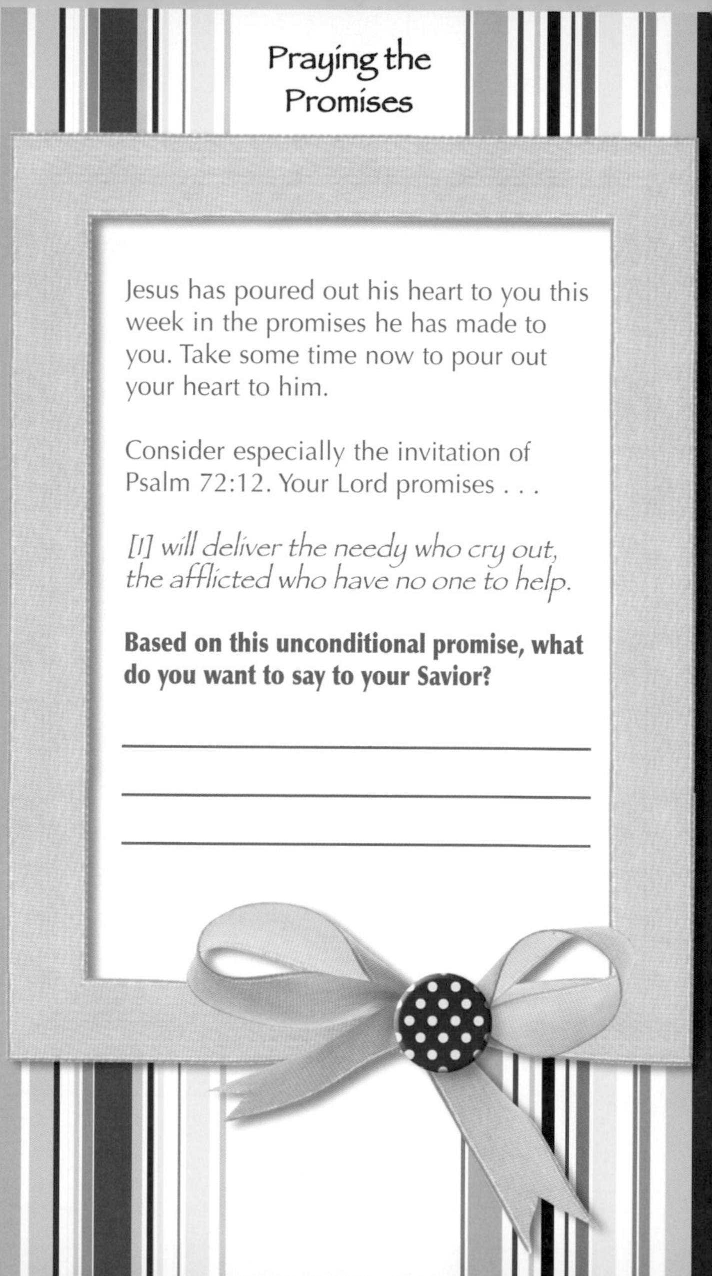

Praying the Promises

Jesus has poured out his heart to you this week in the promises he has made to you. Take some time now to pour out your heart to him.

Consider especially the invitation of Psalm 72:12. Your Lord promises . . .

[I] will deliver the needy who cry out,
the afflicted who have no one to help.

Based on this unconditional promise, what do you want to say to your Savior?

____

____

____

A Clean Heart, a Fresh Start

Do-overs! What a great idea! Kids catch on right away but, in general, it takes adults longer to warm up to the idea.

So read carefully this week. God has promised you a clean heart and a fresh start. It's a fabulous promise! And it's yours!

So now, what will you do with it?

Day 6
Rubbing My Nose in It?

If we confess our sins, he is faithful and just and will forgive us our sins and purify us from all unrighteousness.
1 John 1:9

Before the days of animal psychology, especially the Dog Whisperer, house-training a puppy or kitten had very few rules. You watched your pet closely so as to move it outside when nature called. If you missed the cues and the pet had an accident, you rubbed its nose in the resulting mess.

I'm not sure what theory stood behind this method or what it was intended to teach. But the expression, "rubbing my nose in it," has come to describe being shamed and blamed for one's misdeeds.

It would be easy to mistake our Lord's invitation to confess our sins as a shaming and blaming ritual, as a way he "rubs our nose" in our sins. But nothing could be further from the truth. Instead, he intends our confession as a prelude to his reassurance that he will never stop loving us and that he will continue to work in us those thoughts, words, and actions that honor him.

God is faithful; we are not. Morning by morning, fresh mercies fall like dew from heaven on our sin-hardened hearts. Morning by morning, we bring our needs, our failures, and our shame to the cross of our Savior. There we receive the bright hope Jesus' cross made possible. That sure-and-certain hope melts our shame and raises us from the dust to serve our Savior.

God is also just. He could not overlook our rebellion and the brokenness we bring into his once-perfect creation. We are to blame for much of the pain around us. In justice, God must punish sin. But though we are the blameworthy ones, Jesus chose to take our penalty upon himself. He took our blame, leaving us blameless. Ever our gracious friend, our God now credits Jesus' righteousness—his perfection—to our account.

So now, relying on his promises to heal and help us, we bring our shame and blame to our Savior-God. Fearless, we open our hearts. And we receive just what we've been promised—forgiveness and purification in the cross of Christ.

Lord, I come to you humbly, but in hope, to confess . . .

I will forgive their wickedness
and will remember
their sins no more.
Hebrews 8:12

Wickedness. It's a strong term! I admit it—I'm not thrilled to hear it applied to me! An axe murderer? Sure. That crook who stole the life savings of dozens of senior citizens? Yes, of course. But well-mannered ladies like you and me who read devotions day by day from books like this one? "Wicked"?

Sadly, the answer is yes. Sadder still, the only reason we even think to ask the question is that we fail to see ourselves through the clear and holy eyes of our heavenly Father.

We gulp as we try to swallow this truth, but Scripture never flatters us, never downplays the seriousness of our sin to stroke our ego. Rather, the Bible paints a plain—and most unflattering—picture of our condition before God apart from Jesus.

Still, the Holy Spirit's intention is not to insult us. Rather, like a skilled and compassionate physician, he accurately diagnoses our condition so that he can treat and cure it.

Wickedness. It's a grave diagnosis, one that left untreated leads to death—separation from God now and forever. But praise

God, there is a cure! He promises, "I will forgive their wickedness." When I see my gossip, my hateful thoughts, my self-centeredness as the sins they really are, as wickedness before God, then I also see the cure of Calvary is meant for me.

God forgives! In Christ, our sins are gone!

When we forgive, it's almost impossible to forget—particularly if someone's offense has risen to the level of "wickedness" in our eyes. How easily we carry a grudge, even when we don't want to. But God promises to delete the record of our guilt. And he does! He truly remembers our sins no more.

This promise brings us peace, and it makes it possible for us to demonstrate compassion to those around us whose words and actions sometimes hurt us.

So wherever you may have been, whatever you may have done, you can come home—right now! Repent. Confess. And be refreshed in your Savior's never-ending love.

Lord, forgive me for minimizing the seriousness of sin. My wrongdoing led to the death of your only Son. But even as I see my wickedness, open my eyes to see my Savior, too . . .

You forgave the iniquity of your people and covered all their sins.
Psalm 85:2

Have you ever found yourself in an unforgiving relationship? The friend who feels slighted, no matter how many times we apologize. The sister who suddenly turns a cold shoulder and refuses to explain. The spouse whose trust is broken.

Sometimes others forgive our misbehavior, no strings attached. Sometimes, it takes some time before they can bring themselves to that point. Once in awhile, forgiveness never comes. The relationship cannot be restored—at least, not here on earth. Friendship and trust never return.

How different with our heavenly Father. "You forgave the iniquity of your people," the psalmist says, "and covered all their sins." Because of our precious Savior, forgiveness always comes.

In human relationships, the deeper the hurt caused by our offense, the less likely we will be forgiven. Even our best friends may hesitate to cover our wrongdoing under a warm blanket of forgetfulness. This may give us pause. "Is God like that, too? Will he really forgive?" we may wonder.

We remember our unkind thoughts, our thoughtless words, our faithless worries. We know our failures in prayer and the way our minds wander in worship. We recall the patience we could have shown and the help we could have given.

We need not fear. We can banish every doubt. Because Jesus bled and died for us on Calvary's cross, because he emerged victorious from Easter's open tomb, God forgives us—always and forever! This is no wink-wink-nod-nod backroom cover-up, no shady deal worked out by political cronies and crooks. No, Jesus paid our debt. He endured the punishment we deserved.

Now, the forgiveness he earned for us frees us to live in joy and hope. It plants seeds of humility, awe, and reverence in our hearts. It stirs within us the resolve to avoid living any longer in sin. It drives us into our Savior's arms, knowing he is our security, our only safe hiding place—and knowing that whenever we come to him, he opens his heart wide in welcome.

Lord Jesus, you forgive the sins of your people. And so I come to you in holy hope today with my sins and needs . . .

Day 9
No Exceptions

All the prophets testify about him that everyone who believes in him receives forgiveness of sins through his name.
Acts 10:43

It would be hard to find a more inclusive, all-encompassing promise in Scripture. This promise belongs to *everyone* who believes in Jesus Christ. *All* the prophets say so!

Most human beings like to see themselves as exceptional, unique. In our own eyes, at least, we're each one of a kind. The mold that hatched us broke as we emerged from it.

And we do each have a unique mix of God-given talents and abilities. We each follow different paths through life. Even so, we're much more alike than we are different.

If we were to list everything we have in common, our need for the forgiveness of sins would appear at the top of the list. All the prophets testify to that—Old and New Testaments alike.

- *All have turned aside, they have together become corrupt; there is no one who does good, not even one (Psalm 14:3).*
- *We all, like sheep, have gone astray, each of us has turned to his own way (Isaiah 53:6).*
- *All have sinned and fall short of the glory of God (Romans 3:23).*

Everyone, one by one, has declared independence from our Creator. We have tried to live as if God didn't matter all that much. We've lived as if we matter most of all. In doing that, we've made a mess of our lives, a mess in our families, a big mess of the world around us.

Into the middle of our messes, Jesus Christ descended. He became a true human being—a true human baby, to be precise. He grew up with all the temptations, pains, and problems we ourselves face—yet he remained faithful to God, fully obedient to him. Then he died a cruel death in our place, emerging triumphant over death itself on the first Easter morning.

Jesus did all that so the promise Peter proclaimed in Acts 10 would be fulfilled:

Everyone who believes in him receives forgiveness of sins through his name.

You're no exception—and neither am I. From God's heart to ours—forgiveness!

Lord, your promises to forgive are over the top! How can I begin to thank you for your kindness? Lead me . . .

If you forgive men when they sin against you, your heavenly Father will also forgive you.
Matthew 6:14

In decades past, it became popular to scoff at the idea we should forgive those who hurt us. Psychologists with impressive credentials wrote books trying to discredit the importance of forgiving our enemies. Now, forgiveness is all the rage! Counselors of every stripe recommend it as the way to health, well-being, and peace. Of course, willingness to forgive others has always been one of Christianity's key teachings.

That doesn't mean forgiving others has always—or ever!—been easy. The difficulty posed by it may be one reason the New Testament so often repeats the admonition to forgive.

Forgiveness just doesn't come naturally. We'd rather keep score, tracking the offenses of others against us. Nursing a grudge can feel rather pleasant, at least for a while. Eventually, though, grudges have a way of growing until, monsterlike, the bitterness we've created devours us.

Our Savior teaches us a better way:

For if you forgive men when they sin against you, your heavenly Father will also forgive you.

Almost always when Scripture urges us to forgive, it reminds us in the same breath that our Lord has forgiven us. By forgiving others, we demonstrate that we have understood our need for God's forgiveness—and treasure it. God's forgiveness toward us nurtures and encourages within us the decision to forgive those around us.

Our Savior's goal for each of us is that we become more and more like him—"little Christs," as some have put it. But he will not force that upon us.

Maybe you had a well-meaning parent or first-grade teacher who pressured you and a friend with words like these:

"Say you're sorry!"
"Now say you forgive her!"

Adults can force children to mumble words of confession and forgiveness, but God expects and instills more in his children. As we grow in grace, we come to recognize more and more fully the value of the pardon we have received from Jesus. Then, more and more willingly we pray, "Lord, work your heart of kindness in me and teach me to forgive."

Lord Jesus, your cross laid to rest all the grievances you had against me. Thank you! In light of your pardon, teach me . . .

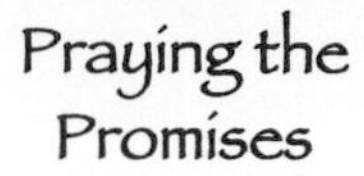

The promise of God's mercy and grace toward us outshines every other promise Scripture makes. Christ's cross and the forgiveness that flows from it make all other promises from God possible.

As you think about Jesus' promise of pardon today, plan a way to respond. Perhaps you'll phone a friend and apologize. Perhaps you'll find a way to make amends for a hurt you caused decades ago. Use the lines below to jot down the possibilities, and then pick one to carry out.

___

___

___

It's All Good!

It's all good! At first blush, that sentence makes me want to shriek in dismay. What about computers that crash—and helicopters that do, too! What about blizzards and botulism and Ebola!

The promises you'll encounter this week don't try to cover up the fact that life is sometimes very hard. But they hold out the hope that our Savior-God is always very good.

We know that in all things God works for the good of those who love him, who have been called according to his purpose.

Romans 8:28

We've titled this chapter "It's All Good!" That phrase has become one of those fads of language like "Where's the beef?" from days of old.

It's all good. Do you agree? Or when you hear these words, do you say to yourself, "Is that so? Then what about . . .?" How would you finish that sentence? What about my diabetes? What about the job (or unemployment) I'm stuck in? What about that flat tire this morning?

Or, more globally, we might ask: What about world poverty? What about dead zones in the ocean? What about the 134 (or so) wars in the world right now?

Our "what-abouts" fly in the face of Paul's words in today's text from Romans. "In all things," the apostle writes, "God works for the good of those who love him." Like the other promises we've been reading, it's yet another inclusive, all-encompassing promise.

Some in our world have corrupted the promise, creating a new expression. "Everything happens for a reason," they say. No.

No, it doesn't. Senseless things happen all the time. We contract lupus. Our boss makes life miserable. Wars mutilate bodies and take lives.

But our Savior-God promises to take even this senselessness and, in mercy, weave it into the fabric of our lives for our good. He promises to do this for "those who love him, who have been called according to his purpose."

Still, as we wait in the rain beside the road for the tow truck, the "what-abouts" may flood our hearts. As we sit in the specialist's waiting room, palms sweating, the "what-abouts" may taunt us. As we watch the latest news alert on TV, the "what-abouts" may threaten to steal our confidence.

But we need not give in to them. "We *know*," Paul writes, inspired by the Holy Spirit himself! Here's what we know:

In all things God works for the good of those who love him, who have been called according to his purpose.

Lord, thank you for the encouragement of this promise. Still, I need your help today with a "what-about" . . .

"No weapon forged against you will prevail, and you will refute every tongue that accuses you. This is the heritage of the servants of the LORD, and this is their vindication from me," declares the LORD. (Isaiah 54:17)

My friend and her husband were being sued. They had done nothing wrong. In fact, they had acted with only one motive in mind—helping! It didn't matter. The subpoenas and depositions, court dates and continuences swept into their lives like a flood. Half-truths, dark hints, and outright untruths threatened to torpedo the small business they had spent a lifetime building.

One evening as a number of us gathered for home Bible study, my friend's fears and frustrations came pouring out. As we prayed together, someone found and read Isaiah 54:17:

> *No weapon forged against you will prevail, and you will refute every tongue that accuses you.*

That's good news to anyone who has ever been unjustly accused. It encourages anyone who has ever been the butt of office gossip or who has lost a promotion because someone fed lies into the rumor mill. It's good news to anyone whose heart has been crushed by life's unfairness in all its forms.

It's even better news to those of us who sometimes find ourselves facing the accusations of a guilty conscience or who struggle when Satan tries to indict us. (It's no accident his name means "the accuser" or "the slanderer"!)

We are, in truth, guilty. And yet, in the cross of our Savior, our Father's promise stands: "You will refute every tongue that accuses you." This promise takes our breath away—or it will when we hear what God is telling us!

Even when the indictment is true, we will refute all charges! It won't take a 1,000-page deposition, either! Four little words will do it: Jesus died for me.

In this world, justice sometimes fails. In heaven's court, though, justice always prevails. Our Father knows and tells the truth about us. He will proclaim it throughout all eternity: In Jesus, we are vindicated, righteous, holy.

Lord, assure me that in the cross of my Savior you see only the best in me. Help me trust you to accomplish your holy purposes in my life now and to bring me safely home . . .

Come to me, all you who are weary and burdened, and I will give you rest.
Matthew 11:28

Most of the time, invitations are exclusive. A few people are invited to State Dinners at the White House. The rest of us stand outside the gates. A few people have tickets to the Super Bowl or World Series. The rest of us watch on TV. A few people have direct access to the company president. The rest of us send an e-mail to her assistant and hope for the best.

In light of all the exclusive opportunities in life, Jesus' inclusive invitation falls on our ears like music, like dew in the desert:

Come to me, all you who are weary and burdened, and I will give you rest.

Savor those words—especially the word *all*. Let the invitation roll over and over in your heart. "Come to me," our Savior says. He speaks to "all who are weary and burdened." Does that include you?

Weary goes far beyond needing one good night's sleep. *Burdened* means much, much more than fending off those one or two niggling worries that occasionally pop into our heads.

What wearies and burdens you right now? When we find ourselves in the long, dark tunnel of weariness and burdens, Jesus meets us there. Just think of that! Jesus meets us there—in those dark places, those dark times when we feel lost.

His presence and his promise transform the darkness, making even our weariness and our burdens a blessing. After all, these things have opened our ears and our hearts to his invitation. They drive us into our Savior's embrace.

It's all good. Or, rather, it's good when we let our Savior's words of hope and promise seep through, transforming our pain. It's good when we turn our back on the sins of worry or pride that have led us into a darkness that threatens to crush us. It's good when we trust our Savior's promise to forgive, to heal, to help. It's good when we rest in his all-inclusive love.

Lord Jesus, your love excludes no one. Your grace invites even me to come, to find rest for my weariness. Right now, I'm carrying many burdens and, trusting your promise, I want to lay them down . . .

In this world you will have trouble. But take heart! I have overcome the world.
John 16:33

Not all promises warm the heart:

- "We'll audit you," promises the IRS when taxpayers take too many unusual deductions—legitimate or not.
- "We'll ticket you," promises the highway patrol when motorists fail to fasten their seatbelts.
- "We'll take your dog to the pound," promises Animal Control when that new puppy wiggles through the fence for the second time in a week.

Not all promises warm the heart—and that includes Jesus' promise of trouble in John 16:33:

In this world you will have trouble . . .

As promises go, this one falls under the column labeled "disturbing." Note, though, that these words are not a threat. Our Lord simply states a fact of life, life that on our fallen planet often includes trials, traumas, and turmoil. Shakespeare once wrote about "Double, double toil and trouble . . ."

Some days, weeks, or years, toil and trouble do seem to double down on us. Fraying relationships. Unraveling finances. Workplace worries. Double toil and double trouble seem to be our lot in life. If even Jesus confirms turmoil's inevitability, what hope can we have!?

The hope we need comes from the Lord's second promise, the promise that comes at the end of this same verse:

Take heart! I have overcome the world.

From our Lord's cross and empty tomb flows ample proof that those who cling to Christ in faith simply cannot lose! Victory belongs to us—in life and in death alike. "It's all good," we can say—even when we must shout those words into the sharp wind of life's fiercest storms. Christ has conquered! He lives and reigns, now and forever.

Trusting that Jesus has overcome and that he shares his victory with us makes every promise of our Savior comforting—even his promises of trouble and trials. Our Friend knows how tough life's troubles can get. He understands and empathizes with us. Still, his love and power go much further. They make us victorious, come what may!

My Savior and Friend, you overcame the world. Teach me to "take heart" as right now I face . . .

Day 15
Conduits of Comfort

Now may the Lord of peace himself give you peace at all times and in every way. The Lord be with all of you.
2 Thessalonians 3:16

One of my friends fought breast cancer—and won. Cancer-free for many years, she now volunteers in a breast cancer clinic, counseling and encouraging patients who are battling the disease.

One of my friends fought breast cancer—and lost. She's with Jesus now. In the last months of her life here on earth, her courage and concern for others testified mightily to the peace Christ gives.

Given a choice, most of us would rather avoid cancer altogether. Most of us would also prefer to sidestep doctors and debt, fiascos and fatigue, insomnia and inflation. (I'm not wild about mice, either!)

But God has not promised us a trouble-free life. In fact, the furnace of difficulty can prepare us in unique ways for service. Consider these words of the apostle Paul:

Praise be to the God and Father of our Lord Jesus Christ, the Father of compassion and the God of all comfort, who comforts us in all our troubles, so that we can comfort those in any trouble with the comfort we ourselves have received from God.

2 Corinthians 1:3–4

- The verse does *not* say God sends trouble into our lives so that we can learn to comfort others. It says that God *comforts us* in our troubles so that we can comfort others.
- The verse includes two beautiful names for God—"the Father of compassion" and "the God of all comfort." How reassuring!
- The verse does *not* urge us to pony up comfort for others from inside ourselves. Instead, it points us to the compassionate Christ as the source of the comfort that will bless others who suffer.

All week, we've explored the truth that whatever happens, "It's all good." It's all good because Jesus has promised to work in every situation for the good of those who love him.

One way he does that is by working through us to comfort others. Both my friends found this true, not despite cancer, but because of it. When have you seen our Savior do something similar in your own life?

Lord Jesus, life is often hard. But you are always good. How I need the peace you promise! Work in me . . .

Praying the Promises

Which promise from the past week's readings means the most to you right now? Use the lines below to write a thank-you note to Jesus for making that promise to you.

____

____

____

____

____

____

Now plan a way to share the comfort of this promise with someone who needs to hear it this week!

Never Alone

Do you ever struggle with loneliness? Even very busy people can. And many, many people in our world today do!

This week we will explore a sure cure for loneliness. Soak up your Savior's love as you consider his promise to be with you.

God has said, "Never will I leave you; never will I forsake you."
Hebrews 13:5

You can have 1,000 "friends" on Facebook and still be lonely. Yes, you can! Researchers from the University of Chicago have proven it.

They've also explored the dangers of loneliness. Being chronically lonely can cause as many health problems as high blood pressure, obesity, lack of exercise, or smoking. Who would have thought that?!

It turns out that loneliness causes our bodies to release stress hormones. It interferes with the body's immune function. It impedes cardiovascular efficiency. Lonely adults tend to sleep less efficiently, eat foods higher in fat, and age prematurely. In truth, loneliness acts a lot like a disease!

God created us for relationship—relationship with him and with one another. That's one reason the promise we will explore this week matters so much. "Never will I leave you; never will I forsake you," our Savior says.

Other people leave us all the time. They move to another state to take a job. They come home after work one day and, seemingly out of the blue, demand a divorce. Best friends drift apart. Our children grow up and establish lives of their own. Death snatches loved ones away.

No relationship on this earth is totally secure. But we can rely absolutely and without question on our Lord's promised presence. He will *never* leave us. He will *never* forsake us.

Interestingly, this verse begins:

Keep your lives free from the love of money
and be content with what you have . . .

How easily we can be seduced into thinking money will keep us secure and things will make us happy! Without even realizing it, we can come to rely on 401k accounts or Social Security checks or a steady paycheck to answer our need for peace—the peace only God's presence can provide.

Instead, our Lord offers us the freedom of contentment—contentment in his presence and in the love that flows from the cross of our Savior. That cross towers over every day of our lives, guaranteeing the forgiveness of all our sins and assuring us that our God will keep every promise he has made to us.

Lord, remind me of your presence today and then work contentment in my heart . . .

Give ear and come to me; hear me, that your soul may live. I will make an everlasting covenant with you, my faithful love.
Isaiah 55:3

What's your favorite getaway? A nail salon appointment? A sunny afternoon in your flower garden with a hoe and spade? A candlelight dinner for two? Two weeks on the beach?

We all need to get away at least once in awhile. We all need to take a break—even from people, work, and service we love. If you doubt that or feel a twinge of guilt because of it, consider this:

Then, because so many people were coming and going that they did not even have a chance to eat, [Jesus] said to [the disciples], "Come with me by yourselves to a quiet place and get some rest."
Mark 6:31

We all need to get away at least once in awhile. Jesus himself experienced this when he lived here on earth. He knows what fatigue and overload feel like. And so he invites, "Come to me."

Now that's a getaway—one like no other! When we go to him, we find true rest. In the shadow of his cross, our souls live, truly and forever! In his presence there is only peace, only acceptance, only compassion, only security. We were born to live there, to live forever in his faithful love. It's what his covenant, his promise to claim us and keep us as his own, is all about.

Most resorts and spas require a reservation. Even nail salons schedule appointments. But this get-away is ours for the asking whenever we need it—even on the spur of the moment. Heaven's door stands open: "Give ear and come to me."

Young moms sleep with one ear open for their infant's cry. Moms of teens sleep with one ear open, too, attentive to the return of their son or daughter from the after-game party or out-of-town marching band competition. Love tunes a mom's ears.

Love tunes our ears to our Lord's words of promise, too. Whether we're weary and worried or elated and energized, we can come. Need to get away? Then run into his arms!

Lord, your covenant of faithful love is mine, just as you have promised. You invite me into your presence, so I come . . .

The LORD replied, "My Presence will go with you, and I will give you rest."
Exodus 33:14

As God made this promise to Moses, the people were about to break camp and set off into the wilderness toward the land God had sworn to give to Abraham and his descendents.

For a year they had lived at the foot of Mount Sinai. There God had given them his Law—the Ten Commandments. There he had provided food and water. There he had begun to heal the scars from 400 years of slavery in Egypt.

But now, it was time to move on. Of all the promises God had made, the promise of his presence shone most brightly among them. Can you identify with the people's need for this promise?

- Moses would take them into unfamiliar territory. The path toward that future was totally new to them. Is the road you're on today taking you to a new and unfamiliar place?
- The camp at Sinai felt safe. Its routines were predictable. Manna appeared, morning by morning. Do you wonder (or even worry) about whether your Lord can provide for you as you leave the safety of the familiar?
- While the chores of daily life went on at Sinai, the work there wasn't especially hard. Leaving, though, would

involve carrying everyone's earthly possessions through the desert—the hot, dry, uncomfortable desert. Is God asking you to move forward into tougher challenges, a lifestyle with more hardships?

These questions and many more like them must have welled up in the people's hearts—and Moses' heart, too. Still, when the pillar of cloud representing God's presence lifted and began to move, Moses and his people followed.

We today don't follow a cloud. Instead, we know God's presence among us as we consider Christ's cross and empty tomb. In Jesus, God is truly present, living among us. In Jesus, we receive rest—rest from the guilt of our sin, rest from the need to worry about our future, rest from the loneliness that threatens to engulf us no matter how many friends' phone numbers we have saved on speed dial.

Review the promise of Exodus 33:14 now. Then consider the bulleted questions above in light of it.

Lord, I need to rest. Let's talk . . .

Day 19
Joy in God's Presence Forever

You have made known to me the path of life; you will fill me with joy in your presence, with eternal pleasures at your right hand. (Psalm 16:11)

Maybe you remember the old expression, "She wants to have her cake and eat it, too." Here's another way to say it: "You can't have it both ways."

It applies, for example, to someone who for weeks demands the impossible from her family. She expects everyone to clean and bake feverishly for a special event, and then wonders why her exhausted helpers don't celebrate with her guests late into the night.

You can't have your cake and eat it, too.

But notice the psalm verse printed at the top of this page. Do you see the past, present, *and* future implications there? Turns out, sometimes you *can* have your cake and eat it, too! God himself promises! And he makes it possible:

- At some point in the past, he planted our feet firmly on the "path of life," the path of true faith. We would never have found that path ourselves as we wandered through life's wilderness. Jesus searched for us and brought us home to life in his family, his church, here on earth.

- Throughout our earthly lives, he will continue to fill us with joy in his presence. Regardless of how we feel at any given moment, regardless of whether we happily eat birthday cake or choke down the dry bread of grief, our Lord's presence buoys our hopes and calms our anxieties.
- Our eyelids will one day close in death, but that will not end our pleasure in God's presence. Instead, we will experience even fuller joys, joys we can't even imagine now. We'll inherit the "eternal pleasures" of God's presence—all because of the life, death, and resurrection of our Savior.

Does all that fill your heart with wonder? God's promise to fill us with joy in his presence is a promise not to be missed!

Lord, as I look back on my life, I see the sustaining power of your presence. As I think about your presence in my life today, my heart overflows. And as for your promise of future joy, I'm at a loss for words . . .

Let us come before him with thanksgiving and extol him with music and song.
Psalm 95:2

Layered lemon dessert.

Layered pudding delight with cherry sauce.

Layered chocolate anything! (Is your mouth watering yet?)

The thing about layered desserts is that, as the cook, you just keep piling on the goodies. God's promises are a little like that, too. All week, we've been exploring the promises of his presence recorded for us in the Holy Scriptures. Now, as we think about our response to these promises, the verse that suggests an appropriate response to that promise adds a dollop of whipped cream and a cherry!

Reread Psalm 95:2. Did you catch it? Not only does Scripture promise us God's presence, it also invites us to come—to come intentionally—into his presence. Think of that! You're invited!

Of course, God is present everywhere, all the time. But he invites us to come into his presence on purpose, responding to his goodness in our lives, especially his goodness to us in

Jesus, our Savior. We can come, as the psalm says, "with thanksgiving . . . with music and song."

What's behind this invitation? Does the God of the universe need our worship? Absolutely not! He invites us because we need to do it!

- As we worship, he reminds us of his forgiveness and his love for us.
- As we worship, he works his Word more deeply into our hearts so that it can strengthen and encourage us.
- As we worship, he assures us we're not alone. He's present with us—and we belong to his family.

The brothers and sisters who worship beside us share our faith. They pray for us and with us. With them, we get to live out what someone has called the "one another verses" of the New Testament. Here are a few:

- *By this all men will know that you are my disciples, if you love one another (John 13:35).*
- *Be devoted to one another in brotherly love (Romans 12:10).*
- *Live in harmony with one another (Romans 12:16).*
- *Serve one another in love (Galatians 5:13).*

Lord, your promises add layer upon layer of blessings to my life. As I worship with your people, please . . .

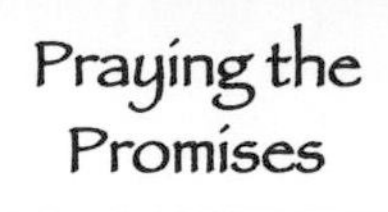

All week, we've considered our Lord's many promises to be with us always. And we've thought about ways to respond to those promises—in worship and by participating more fully in the family of God.

Think a little more about that now, jotting practical plans for the next few weeks on the lines below. Think especially about ways to serve people who may be lonely—shut-ins, busy single moms, the recently widowed.

Forever Trustworthy

Past. Present. Future.

God's promises are sure, no matter where you stand in history, no matter what your stage in life.

The Scriptures you will explore this week are well worth scrutinizing and well worth memorizing.

May Jesus bless your quest!

No matter how many promises God has made, they are "Yes" in Christ. And so through him the "Amen" is spoken by us to the glory of God.
2 Corinthians 1:20

Do you think of *yes* as a happy word? In general, *yes* creates joy when it answers questions like these:

- I've found my dream house! Do I qualify for a loan?
- Did you get the job?
- Will you marry me?
- Did the university's acceptance letter come?
- Will you publish my book?

In each case, *yes* comes only after we've cleared major hurdles, completed demanding tasks. We clean up our credit record. We do our homework. We attend a rigorous trade school. We write and rewrite and rewrite the manuscript yet again.

In contrast, God's promises to us are *yes* in Jesus, *yes* because of what he did, not because of what we have done or will do.

In Christ, God forgives. In Christ, God is with us forever. In Christ, every challenge we face becomes a blessing. In Christ, all our needs are fully met. In Christ, all the many promises God has made are fulfilled.

That's one reason we pray "in Jesus' name." The formula isn't some magical incantation. Instead, it reminds us that in and of ourselves, we have no claim on God or his blessings. As sinners, forgiven in our Savior, we come to God, asking him to fulfill his promises because of what Jesus has done for us.

This brings us to the end of today's verse:

And so through him the "Amen" is spoken by us to the glory of God.

Through Christ, enfolded by his love for us, we can say "Amen" to every one of God's promises. Most importantly, we can say "Amen" to that specific promise we need to claim right now. The Hebrew word *amen* means, "Yes, so be it" or "Yes, it shall be so."

This word, placed at the end of our prayers, expresses trust that our promise-making God will do what he has said. And, as Scripture points out, God is glorified.

My Father, when you gave Jesus into death for me, you demonstrated your intention to fulfill all the promises you have made. Still, trust often comes hard . . .

Day 22
Zero Failures

Praise be to the LORD, who has given rest to his people Israel just as he promised. Not one word has failed of all the good promises he gave through his servant Moses. (1 Kings 8:56)

If you've ever invested in the stock market or even thought about doing so, you can probably recite this disclaimer from memory:

Past performance is no guarantee of future results.

In the stock market, it's absolutely true. In regard to the promises our Lord has made, though, it's a different story altogether. Past performance is a wonderfully reliable guarantee of future results! In fact, past performance is a leading indicator of future results!

Today's Scripture verse comes from a blessing King Solomon spoke over God's people on the day the nation dedicated the temple. By that point in history, Moses had been dead for well over 400 years. God had given his people ample time to observe his trustworthiness. Solomon testifies to what they had experienced:

Not one word has failed of all the good promises he gave through his servant Moses.

What makes Solomon's testimony especially stunning is the fact that during those many years, God's people had chalked up a spotty record in the faith department.

Included in those years were decades spent under the leadership of Joshua and David—on the whole, godly leaders of a godly (yet not sinless) people. But included in those years also were the chaotic, violent centuries in which the judges ruled. Two words summarize those centuries—*idolatrous* and *brutal*.

Yet the golden cord of God's faithfulness winds its way through every day of all those decades and centuries. Not one word of our Lord's good promises had ever failed. He had proven himself fully trustworthy. And he will continue to do that in your life.

Are you counting on specific promises today? Or are you worried that your faithlessness or disobedience might have voided God's promises to you? Then turn in repentant faith to the cross of your Savior. Confess your sins and cling to his promise to forgive and cleanse you from all unrighteousness (1 John 1:9). Then claim all the other promises you need as well. They are yours in Jesus.

Father-God, you are always faithful. Your promises never fail. So now . . .

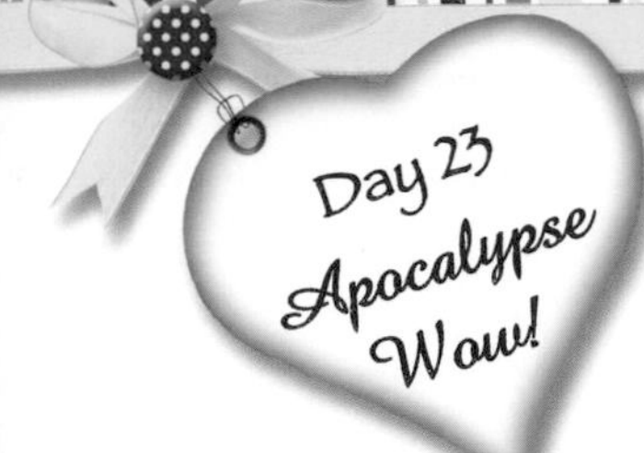

The grass withers and the flowers fall, but the word of our God stands forever.
Isaiah 40:8

Disaster movies sell. Those of us old enough to remember *The Poseidon Adventure* easily recall the moment a giant wave capsized the Poseidon, an opulent ocean liner, turning it completely upside down in the midst of the ocean.

By someone's count, Hollywood has dramatized . . .

- 11 major motion pictures devoted to avalanche disasters
- 21 films featuring earthquake devastation
- 9 movies focusing on impending meteor or asteroid bombardments of our planet
- 20 films featuring volcanic upheavals
- 23 blockbusters depicting floods and tidal waves
- 57 movies about various climate and weather disasters, including tornadoes, hurricanes, and global warming

That's a lot of footage devoted to destruction, especially since this list omits all the films about man-made disasters like epidemics and nuclear war.

Interestingly, though, none of them ends in Earth's demise. Every time, humanity survives, though often it's hanging by a thread.

If nothing else, movies like these remind us how fragile life is and how little control we really have over our own futures. One lightning strike, one slip of the bedrock along a fault line, one stray meteor from outer space, and life as we know it is toast.

Even if no major disaster mars our lifetime, little by little, smaller events can and do change our lives forever. Isaiah was right: "The grass withers and the flowers fall." Happily, though, he was right about something else, too: "The word of our God stands forever."

Someday, our Lord himself will call a halt to life on earth as we know it. Jesus will descend . . .

. . . with a loud command, with the voice of the archangel and with the trumpet call of God, and the dead in Christ will rise.
1 Thessalonians 4:16

But even that won't spell an end to the promises God has made to his people. His word "stands forever." Jesus' promised (and, thus, certain) return will usher in endless peace and joy for all who trust in him as Savior. We will experience at last the fullness of the promises he has made.

Amen! Come, Lord Jesus!

Lord, your word stands forever. Work in me . . .

Day 24
No Lie!

. . . a faith and knowledge resting on the hope of eternal life, which God, who does not lie, promised before the beginning of time. (Titus 1:2)

Remember the taunt from childhood? "Liar, Liar, pants on fire!" It seems silly now, but when we were seven or eight, those words stung.

As the apostle Paul begins his letter to the young pastor Titus, he strikes a note of encouragement, reminding Titus of the eternal life God has promised his people. Paul includes this little phrase to describe the faithful One who makes the promise: "God, who does not lie."

No one can walk into heaven's throne room chanting, "Liar, Liar . . ." Underscoring the fact that eternal life comes to sinners as God's gift and not because of anything we have done, Paul wrote elsewhere (Romans 3:4):

Let God be true, and every man a liar.

No matter how hard we argue our own case or try to make ourselves look meteoric, Scripture makes it clear. God is true, even though we often deceive ourselves about our own worthiness. Salvation comes always and only by grace through faith in Christ the crucified—just as God promised.

The verse from Titus contains another golden nugget to underscore this. Reread it now, paying particular attention to the timing of the promise. When did God make it?

. . . a faith and knowledge resting on the hope of eternal life, which God, who does not lie, promised before the beginning of time.

Interesting. "Before the beginning of time" neither you nor I were around. No human being was. So, to whom did God make the promise to rescue his people from sin and death, the promise to give us eternal life? Who but himself?! This further reinforces the certainty of that promise.

We may at times be faithless. We may at times reject the knowledge of God to pursue the trivialities and trinkets this world offers. But our Savior-God is faithful. He will always forgive his repentant children for the sake of Jesus. He will always heal and restore.

Father, you kept your promise to open the way to eternal life and you will keep every other promise, too. I'm so often faithless. Father, forgive! Then work . . .

Day 25
Pure, Perfect, Holy

Since we have these promises, dear friends, let us purify ourselves from everything that contaminates body and spirit, perfecting holiness out of reverence for God.
2 Corinthians 7:1

In August of 1926, Gertrude Ederle swam the English Channel in 14 hours and 31 minutes. She broke the men's record for this 21-mile swim by nearly two hours, though some controversy still swirls around her feat.

Forty-six years later, 15-year-old Lynne Cox broke all previous channel-swimming records, making her way across in 9 hours, 57 minutes. She was also the youngest person ever to swim the English Channel. To top it off, she returned a year later to shatter her own record in a 9-hour, 36-minute effort.

Swimming the English Channel ranks near the top of human athletic endeavors. In difficulty, it rivals climbing Mount Everest, finishing Hawaii's Ironman Triathlon, and competing in the Olympic decathlon. Only the world's greatest athletes need apply. The rest of us sit on the sidelines, muttering the word "impossible" to ourselves.

Reading 2 Corinthians 7:1 can evoke the same response. Only super-Christians need apply:

Since we have these promises, dear friends, let us purify ourselves from everything that contaminates body and spirit, perfecting holiness out of reverence for God.

Really? "Perfecting holiness"? Yes. And the verse tells us how in two steps.

Step 1—We have "these promises" to cheer us on. Everything God has done for us and promises to continue doing encourages us to keep on going. His promise to forgive our failures stands at the top of the list. Knowing the sacrifice our Savior made for us on his own bloody cross, we respond in joyful obedience.

Step 2—We have "reverence for God" to strengthen our resolve. This holy fear, planted by the Holy Spirit himself, leads us to hate our sins more and more. And it strengthens us for the fight against temptation.

This side of the finish line, perfect holiness will elude us. Day by day, moment by moment, we rely on our Father's faithful love and forgiveness. But he will complete his work in us as we snap the tape and cross into eternity. What a promise! What a Savior!

Lord, your promises cheer me on! Continue to work in me . . .

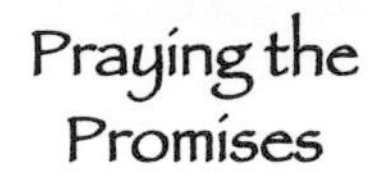

Over the past five weeks, you've encountered many promises from the God of the universe—the God who also happens to be your Father and Savior in Jesus. These promises have the power to revolutionize your life!

So before you walk away, think about what you've read. What do you want to say to your Lord about it? What changes do you want him to work? Jot some notes about that on the lines below. Then incorporate your thoughts into a prayer—one that may begin an ongoing conversation with your Lord!

More Promises from God's Heart to Yours

Scripture contains almost too many promises to count. Here are a few of them. As you read your Bible in the days and weeks ahead, look for these and others, and then highlight them!

I tell you the truth, he who believes has everlasting life. (John 6:47)

My sheep listen to my voice; I know them, and they follow me. I give them eternal life, and they shall never perish; no one can snatch them out of my hand. (John 10:27-28)

I am the resurrection and the life. He who believes in me will live, even though he dies. (John 11:25)

I am the vine; you are the branches. If a man remains in me and I in him, he will bear much fruit; apart from me you can do nothing. (John 15:5)

The LORD himself goes before you and will be with you; he will never leave you nor forsake you. Do not be afraid; do not be discouraged.

(Deuteronomy 31:8)

To see all of CTA's books, visit us at www.CTAinc.com.

If this book has made a difference in your life or if you have simply enjoyed it, we would like to hear from you. Your words will encourage us!

We invite you to post your comments at share.ctainc.com.

Or you can reach us at:

Editorial Manager,
Department GPW1SC
CTA, Inc.
PO Box 1205
Fenton, MO 63026-1205

or by e-mail at editor@CTAinc.com.
Please include the subject line: GPW1SC.